Raquel de la Cruz Díaz Sánchez
Axel Francisco Orozco Torres
Ramón Gerardo Navejas Padillla

Judo, a pedagogical resource to prevent crime.

Raquel de la Cruz Díaz Sánchez
Axel Francisco Orozco Torres
Ramón Gerardo Navejas Padillla

Judo, a pedagogical resource to prevent crime.

Perceptions and challenges.

ScienciaScripts

Imprint

Cover image: www.ingimage.com

This book is a translation from the original published under ISBN 978-620-3-03367-0.

Publisher:
Sciencia Scripts
is a trademark of
Dodo Books Indian Ocean Ltd., member of the OmniScriptum S.R.L Publishing group
str. A.Russo 15, of. 61, Chisinau-2068, Republic of Moldova Europe
Printed at: see last page
ISBN: 978-620-3-21385-0

Judo, High Performance Sports as a Pedagogical Resource for Crime Prevention, in Colonia Constitución, Zapopan, Jalisco, perceptions and challenges.

Judo High Performance Sport as a Pedagogical resource for Crime Prevention, in Colonia Constitución, Zapopan, Jalisco, perceptions and challenges.

Mtra. Raquel de la Cruz Díaz Sánchez***
Primary School María Teresa Calderón Velasco
raqueldsjudo@gmail.com

Dr. Axel Francisco Orozco Torres**
University of Guadalajara Centro Universitario de Los Valles
axel.orozco@academicos.udg.mx

Coordinator Dr. Ramon Gerardo Navejas Padilla
University of Guadalajara
Centro Universitario de Los Valles
ramon.navejas@academicos.udg.mx

Content

1.- Summary

The commitment to security is one of the shared responsibilities in a society, mainly for the prevention of crime and integration of the social fabric, more so when there are civil institutions that are in a "dynamic process" (Sahagún, 2008), to achieve citizenship, especially when state institutions are not interested in working on long-term politics as is the case in our society where politicians and top-level authorities seek short-term programs with results that give them bonuses.

The Dojo "Kodomo Nobasho with more than 20 years (Diaz, 2019), is dedicated to the study and training of Judo as a high performance sport; this institution receives in its ranks children with school problems of behavior and character to seek in them obtain community identity and their "belonging to a family to a social community (Sahagun, 2008)", following the values of Kodokan from the paradigm of Jigoro Kano founder of Judo, and the approach of competitions as:

> "Mobilization of knowledge, skills, attitudes and values, as well as their capacities and experiences that an individual makes in a specific context, to solve a problem or situation that is presented to him in the different areas of his life" (Government of Mexico, 2020).

This is how Kodomo from sport and science, participates with a vision from sociology and education to criminal policy mainly from the prevention of crime as an action a participatory citizen preserving and providing; "Strengthening the life skills of young people is a key objective to minimize risk factors and maximize protection factors related to crime (UNODC, 2019)", all this without leaving aside, as it has been said, "their kinship with the humanities (Merton, 2002)" in the face of common threats, building bridges between sport and crime prevention.

1.- Abstract:

The commitment to security is one of the responsibilities shared in a society, mainly for crime prevention and integration of the social fabric, especially when there are civil institutions that are in a "dynamic process (Sahagun, 2008)", to achieve citizenship, especially when state institutions do not have the interest to work long- term politics as in our society where politicians and top-level authorities seek short- term programs with results that grant them bonuses.

The Dojo "Kodomo Nobasho with more than 20 years (Díaz, 2019)", is dedicated to the study and training of Judo as a high performance sport; This institution receives in its ranks children with school behavior and character problems to seek in them to obtain community identity and their "belonging to a family to a social community (Sahagún, 2008)", following the Kodokan values from the paradigm of Jigoro Kano founder of Judo, and the competency approach as:

> "Mobilization of knowledge, skills, attitudes and values, as well as their abilities and experiences that an individual performs in a specific context, to solve a problem or situation that is presented in the different areas of their life" (Government of Mexico, 2020).

This is how Kodomo from sports and science participates with a vision from sociology and education to criminal policy mainly from crime prevention as an action a participatory citizen preserving and providing; "Strengthening the life skills of young people is a key objective to minimize risk factors and maximize protection factors related to crime (UNODOC, 2019)", all this without neglecting as stated " their relationship with the humanities (Merton, 2002) "in the face of common threats, forging bridges between sport and crime prevention.

2.- Keywords: Judo, prevention, crime, perception, security.2.- Keywords: Judo, prevention, crime, perception, security.

3.- Introduction:

The figure of the citizen, often separates us from reality and even see the abnormal as normal, such is the case of violence and crime, so it is of paramount importance to have programs that lead to educate about skills and values in times of turmoil, but that lead to educate especially in prevention, prevention should be the bet of society. Some of the social tendencies can be seen as a latent threat where the rhythm of life allows us to make a space of reflection; the insecurity and the perspectives of education of the young people and of our society before the abandonment and discrimination of all type, makes us observe spaces of encounter where the contact with the young people and the children appreciate moments of joy, enthusiasm, confidence, sincerity and authenticity present in this stage of the life.

For this work, the research processes were respected and the pertinent permissions were requested. This is a qualitative vision where Judo, High Performance Sport as a Pedagogical resource for the Prevention of Crime, in Colonia Constitución, Zapopan, Jalisco, perceptions and challenges are approached, which were methodologically reviewed with technique and methodological strategies respecting at all times the reliability and validity of the study in question by systematically addressing and documenting the records obtained.

This work can be taken as an applicable proposal to prevent crime, creating a bridge between pedagogy, sports, formal/informal education and crime prevention, since under this context a theoretical framework is addressed that provides a path for research from a different perspective that could lead to criminal policy and crime prevention.

4.- Public safety

The concept of public security is regularly associated with the police forces, but according to the Constitution itself, it has major connotations, as stipulated in Article 21, which not only encompasses this area, but also emphatically addresses crime prevention:

> "to safeguard the life, freedoms, integrity and heritage of persons, as well as to contribute to the generation and preservation of public order and social peace, ... Public security includes prevention.
>
> c) The formulation of public policies aimed at preventing the commission of crimes.
>
> d) The participation of the community will be determined, which will help, among others, in the processes of evaluation of the policies of prevention of the crime as well as of the institutions of public safety. (Congress of the Union, 2020)".

However, public security is an area that is failing despite multiple reforms, training, economic and human resources invested in it, considering also the benefits that some of these security forces have acquired, this is how we arrive at two paradigms:

> First, "most Mexicans distrust the police. Eight out of ten said so in the 2010 Latinobarometer survey. The evidence is indisputable, all available surveys confirm this majority distrust (Elizabeth, 2015)".
>
> Second, "Security is one of the situations that cause the greatest concern to citizens (National Electoral Institute-El Colegio de México, 2015)" and according to the World Justice Project report, Rule of Law Index in Mexico for the periods 2018 to 2020, according to the factor 5, Order and Security, point 5.3, which measures citizen perception in its entity and spaces such as the home, work, public spaces, school, and transportation such as the automobile, public transportation, and/or the highway, "in 2018, only 0.45 of the people feel safe and from 2019 to 2020, only 0.5.
> 0.38 feel safe (World Justice Project, report 2018, 2019, 2020)".

In both cases, this leads us to a generalized process of distrust in the actors of public security, a fact that is regrettable for those who live in that entity and that leads us to the redoubt of the city, the neighborhood and the colony, where the citizen becomes sensitive to the problems that he faces on a daily basis due to the emphasis of the events that have occurred in his community and of immediate impact on his family. Public security as such faces various problems, both internal and external, and the analyses that are made about it can even be seen as "out of touch with reality or lacking in content (Felipe, 2007 p.257)," and not exactly because they are poorly elaborated, but rather because of the vices that exist within it:

> "The commanders and their strategies are elaborated according to their knowledge and understanding. They believe that because they were most of their life in a security corps or the army itself they can lead a public security corps without having the slightest capacity or sense of what public security is and as if on the other hand these people belong to historical moments where we know at least in the country, State and municipalities the old police were always corrupt and now you see them running these bodies has but also defend themselves "when they have found something" no, they will not find them because the citizen is always afraid to point them out because they crucify him so now to participate is very complicated and their programs the same but they never check if they are good, if they give results but they give their programs even if they do not serve and do not see other things they are always right so are the politicians and those who put in those positions (5, 2019).

So this vision of the members of public security from the inside and due to the public perception, public security is a complex pending for politicians, the State and the citizens.

However, since "Article 3 Every individual has the right to life, liberty and security of person (Universal Declaration of Human Rights, 1948)", which leads us to point out and resignify public security seen as it has been done at the moment and debate it as a right to security of citizens, which also leads us to review the social aspects that must be allow a full development of these, which is adopted for the purposes of this work from the processes of informal education, to seek the welfare and development of athletes in their social and family environment with a climate of belonging from the vision of citizens and a specific place, resignifying the concepts of public safety and public security. Thus, the Inter-American Commission on Human Rights presented a report approved by the Inter-American Commission on Human Rights on December 31, 2009, in which point two of its Executive Summary states

> "Citizen security is one of the dimensions of human security and therefore of human development and involves the interrelationship of multiple actors, conditions and factors, including the history and structure of the state and society; government policies and programs; the enforcement of economic, social and cultural rights; and the regional and international scenario. Citizen security is threatened when the state does not fulfill its function of providing protection against crime and social violence, which interrupts the basic relationship between those who govern and those who are governed (Report on Citizen Security and Human Rights, 2009).

From this, it is worth noting that the evolution from public security to citizen security is charged with a multidisciplinary note considering citizen participation and their human rights, with emphasis on public policies of prevention; having the citizen and his participation under two central axes "normative, relative to the absence of threats. On the other hand, it refers to social practices (Elizabeth, 2015)". Taking into account mainly social practices, prevention through sport is present, considering also another new paradigm, that of "social fabric" under two aspects:

> 1. "The relative: It is the nexus that people form by blood relations or mutual nucleus that coexists daily, these are: grandparents, parents, children, siblings, aunts and uncles, nephews, cousins and others. They need each other to meet needs or help each other.
>
> 2. The community: Born from different family nuclei that live very close together to form a community (Habitat for Humanity in Mexico, 2018)".

Being then for the case that occupies us the second one, which we find in the group of young athletes and families, united by a process of informal education linked to the "Judo" as sport of high Olympic performance, looking for the prevention of the crime and the reconstruction of the social fabric through them in the Colonia Constitución in Zapopan; Jalisco.

4.1 Crime Prevention

The prevention of crime and delinquency is a component of the discourse in many of the strategies of public security, as a consequence of the social processes that a neighborhood or colony lives mainly of delinquency and social disorganization that can have incidence in the individuals in particular taking them to processes of crisis due to the environment according to Edwin Sutherland, quoted by Tieghi "the criminal behavior is always a result of learning (TIEGHI, 1989 Págs. 388-389), hence the nine main principles or ideas with which he maintains that the process of behavior is learned according to the environment, which may be that of crime, or that of prevention in a process of disorganization:

1. Criminal behavior is learned.
2. You learn in interaction with other subjects through the process of communication.
3. The main part of the learning process, i.e. the one in which the criminal behavior is acquired, takes place within the individual's most intimate relationships with his or her family and friends.
4. Learning about criminal behavior includes learning about the techniques of committing the crime, as well as the specific orientation of motives, impulses, attitudes and the very rationalization of criminal behavior.
5. The specific direction of motives and impulses is learned from the most varied definitions of legal precepts, favorable or unfavorable to them.
6. A person becomes a criminal when the definitions in favor of violation of the law outweigh the unfavorable ones (because of his differential contacts he learned more criminal ways than law-abiding ones).
7. The differential associations of the individual can be different according to the frequency, duration, priority and intensity of the same.

8. The learning process corresponds to that of all the mechanisms inherent in any learning process.
9. Although criminal behavior is an expression of general needs and values, it cannot be explained as a concretion of those needs and values, since conduct in accordance with the law also responds to identical needs and values (García-Pablo de Molina, 1988, pp. 557-559).

With this proposal, it is understood that criminal policy should seek to optimize the development of good social conditions and social stability, models of learning from the cell of society, the family, that is, we are talking about a process of citizenship in which the government is occupied in its true functions, and that politicians do not empower themselves with their party or personal interests but rather empower the social fabric, according to "Sutherland starts from the general consideration that social disorganization is the cause of crime and that consequently a better social organization will decrease criminality (Orellana Wiarco, 2007)".

However, the Chicago school should be highlighted, which turns to reality to interpret it and generate knowledge from the objects of study as a preponderant value for concrete decision making on social problems, also known as urban sociology, with "systematic field work as instruments for the interpretation of aspects of social reality in the search for approximation (Azpúrua Gruber, vol. 6, no. 2, July-December, 2005,)".

This is how we can have an approach to the concept of prevention, which impacts on the life of a society and their families from the various environments and situations that generate risk factors that are, "variables that can negatively affect the development of people (W, refurbished March 2020)" therefore having multiple strategies to reduce or modify these processes which can be classified into six areas.

1. **"Individual factors:** low IQ, poor conflict resolution skills, favorable attitudes and values towards

risk behaviors (concept explained in point 3), hyperactivity, difficult temperament in childhood.

2. **Family factors:** low family cohesion, having mentally ill parents, coercive, ambivalent or permissive parenting styles
3. **Factors linked to the peer group:** belonging to peer groups involved in risky activities (criminal behavior, drug use, for example)
4. **School factors:** low teacher support, school alienation, school violence
5. **Social or community factors:** low community support, stigmatization and exclusion from community activities
6. **Socio-economic and cultural factors:** living in poverty (W, refurbished March 2020)".

All these phenomena are associated with unemployment, inequalities between different geographical sectors, precarious or disorganized schools, deficiencies in formal and informal education, low levels of performance, abandonment and expulsion from schools at various levels, early aggressive behavior or serious substance abuse, others such as severe or erratic parenting, violence, poverty, isolation, relationships with friends and peers that encourage young people to take risks and break the law, knowing these factors allows for the multiple risk factors that prevention programs can be directed to neighborhoods or colonies at high risk.

Just as there are risk factors, we also have protective factors that support the consolidation of an environment of risk resistance in the subjects. What many times becomes complex because here we would suppose that they exist;

> "well-governed cities with low levels of inequality and effective and equitable authorities... adequate funding for social programs, ...and citizen participation (UNODOC/United Nations Office on Drugs and Crime/International Center for the Prevention of Crime, 2011)".

For this reason, it is extremely important to have adequate and solid formal-informal education processes, as well as recreational areas that provide young people with diverse options that generate opportunities with human resources, promoting processes of resistance to crime through consolidated mainly focused on the development of the subject as well as social factors and the community, this is where four paradigms of social intervention stand out;

1. "Crime prevention through social development; ...highlighting school-based education projects or recreational and training projects for children and youth in communities, also as an attempt to increase awareness and resilience as they grow and develop.
2. Local or community-based crime prevention; ... increase services as well as capital or social cohesion in the community. Social capital" is often understood to mean the network of social relationships, mutual trust and shared values, community solidarity, or sense of civic identity that exists in a neighborhood. It involves the active participation of the population and local organizations in the communities and neighborhoods concerned.
3. Prevention of crime-friendly situations; includes approaches that aim to reduce people's opportunities to commit crime, increase the risks and costs of being arrested and minimize the benefits to the offender. Five specific categories of crime-friendly strategies have been defined: "Those that increase offenders' efforts" "Those that increase offenders' risks" "Those that reduce offenders' earnings" "Those that reduce incitement to offend" "Those that remove excuses for offending.12 Situational techniques are designed to be applied to very specific forms of crime and assume that potential offenders make rational decisions about the potential risks and benefits of breaking the law.
4. Social reintegration programs. Crime prevention through social reintegration refers to all programmes aimed at children, youth or adults already involved in the criminal justice system, including those in detention and those returning to the community (UNODOC/United Nations Office on Drugs and Crime/International Centre for the Prevention of Crime, 2011)".

From the epidemiological approach we find three levels:

1) "Primary prevention aimed at the general population and, commonly, responds to non-specific needs, acting on the social and situational contexts that favor violence.
2) Secondary prevention aimed at specific risk groups and their needs (children, youth or women), who have already had a problem as a result of violence and who require treatment and support to avoid re-victimization, or to prevent them from becoming future victimizers.

3) Tertiary prevention is aimed at specific groups of people who have committed law violations, who have entered the criminal system, seeking to promote their rehabilitation (Universidad de Chile/Open Society Institute/Centro de Estudios en Seguridad Ciudadana, 2004)".

As can be seen, the scenario is modified according to each of the phenomena in which society itself actively participates. The responsibility no longer falls or should fall to the State alone, but it should also know how to respond to the needs of the community, collective society or civic associations, of its organized groups, in general so that they participate proactively in the design of prevention strategies according to the different phenomena and approaches that require in many cases commitment, constancy, economic investment of human resources that can even last several years, For this reason, this type of work is stoic in the face of the difficulties faced in this type of work, whether with the community, due to the lack of economic and human resources, or with the government, and of course, with those to whom this type of program is directed, This is especially true when the state itself does not participate and finally observes the results of this type of grouping and considers that it was a short term effort to take control of the strategies or make them their own without effort because the results are favorable or politically dress the group in power, hence the great dichotomy and lack of interest on the part of these communities in participating with the government.

4.1.2 Education and Sports

When we talk about education and sport, we find ourselves in the need to talk about socio-educational intervention, in which we will find diverse actors and scenarios, as well as by their intentionality, strategies and mainly because it leads us to a transformation action under the paradigm of a dynamic or reality about a community, through projects in this case of areas such as formal-informal education and sport for crime prevention. For better understanding the place you want to reach and define sport from a crime prevention perspective is taken from the SAR's definition:

"**1.** m. Physical activity, exercised as a game or competition, whose practice involves training and subject to rules (Real Academica de la Lengua Española, 2020)", under this tenor then we can point out that a sport promotes not only the physical and entertainment aspects but also values, which is linked in an integral way as one of its important characteristics for the good development of the human being, under the paradigm of a formative pedagogy. Thus the acquisition of attitudes through sport is the result that comes from the development of the work that is done under the expression of behaviors with emphasis on the sport that is practiced, taking the subjects to a second moment that would be the initiation of sport that deals mainly with:

> "a motor content with important educational values: stage in which one or several people start learning, in a playful way, the generic and specific skills needed to start practicing one or several sports, developing their physical condition in a healthy way, learning progressively the basic rules of the sport modality being carried out, favoring a positive attitude towards the practice of physical activity, and promoting a true education in values (Giménez Fuentes-Guerra & Rodríguez López, 2006)".

With such a definition, there is an approach to the processes that should prevail in society in this case through sport, so the social fabric in which a subject lives will feed him through a healthy environment, of leisure and informal education linking him to a space of learning in behaviors with values necessary in every society as Akers points out "The family, groups of friends, schools, churches, and other groups offer the most immediate contexts that promote or hinder criminal behavior in accordance with the rules (Akers, 1997 p. 69)", however if it is a sport that motivates subjects without exception with great or small achievements, it begins to promote the habits of sport but also values, so it is essential that this type of program has an extra, and that this extra can only be given by enjoying the sport itself and motivation that athletes and their coaches have, also there are various causes of abandonment of sport or demotivation as is the lack of economic resources, parents do not see in their children an athlete and only seek to have their children in an extracurricular activity that "entertain them or waste their time doing something and are not alone at home (family, 2018)", also the demand of parents for their children to maintain high rankings in sports, the first causes can be overcome with sports scholarships or support from sponsors or governments themselves when they see the benefits and those close links sport prevention; with the rest of the elements, they are combined in a process that not only prevents the crime but also links the subject as a citizen with his community.

In the psycho-social field, sport provides elements such as

> **"Psychological Qualities" -** knowledge of our possibilities and limitations, spirit of self-improvement, development of self-control and responsibility, self-worth and self-esteem, motivation
>
> **Educational values:** Healthy habits, autonomy, creativity, equality, solidarity, ecology (Giménez Fuentes-Guerra & Rodríguez López, 2006)".

It is possible to point out then that sport contains educational possibilities that go from mobility and corporeity, to a process of affective and social development, from there its importance, because it begins the process where the subject realizes objectives of social character and becomes aware of the others of the other, beginning to integrate itself in society, to reject the improper conducts, by virtue of the respect and sense of responsibility acquired before the others in a process of sport and social interaction.

4.1.3 Judo

Jigoro Kano, who studied at Kyoto University's Faculty of Political Science at the age of 22, founded his first Dojo, a physical space dedicated to the training of the sport; Kodokan was the name adopted by his school, the

Kodokan became the center where Japanese and foreigners went to take judo teachings together and mutual help, so in this way it became one of its philosophical paradigms "Only through mutual help and concessions can an organism that groups individuals in great or small numbers find their full harmony and make serious progress (Ruiza)", also took as an emblem the cherry blossom (*sakura*). As the dean of Tokyo's College of Teacher Training, he was progressive and revolutionary in his approach to the Japanese educational model, allowing students from lower social classes to enter.

Kano, was in fact the first Japanese to belong to the International Olympic Committee from 1912 to 1936, in that process in 1915 he was decorated by King Gustav of Sweden, with the Olympic medal due to his effort to promote with an elevated spirit the sport.

When he retired he dedicated himself to the diffusion of judo, by that time he already had followers, so he came to the celebration of the fiftieth anniversary of the Kodokan, in 1934: "When he died, in 1938, he left a written work, *Kodokan*, in which the foundations of his philosophy were exposed (Ruiza)".

In 1962 a new building was built in Tokyo and by 1964, judo appears as an Olympic discipline in men and it was in the Seoul Olympics, when it was included for women as a competitive sport. Kano, as an educator, was idealistic, especially looking for an educational process through judo. As a writer, among his principles, he stands out in his poems:

1. "EDUCATION There is nothing greater in the world. The moral education of one person extends to ten thousand people. The education of one generation extends to one hundred generations.
2. EDUCATION There is nothing more enjoyable in the world. Cultivating talent and improving the world, this fragrance lives on forever after death (Carlos Gutiérrez García, 2008)".

Likewise, among the principles assumed by Kano, we find that of "maximum efficiency", which as a moral conduct will be developed from the discipline and application of its principles:

> "This principle of maximum efficiency, when applied to the increase or improvement of social life, as well as when applied to the coordination of body and mind... requires, first of all, order and harmony among its members, and this can only be achieved by mutual help and concessions, leading to mutual welfare and benefit.
>
> The final objective of Judo is, therefore, to instill in the mind of man a spirit of respect for the principle of maximum efficiency and of mutual welfare and benefit, leading him to practice them so that man individually and collectively can reach the highest condition...
>
> If we look closely at the present state of society throughout the world, despite the fact that morality in all its forms (religious, philosophical, and traditional) is intended to improve man's conduct in society and make the world ideal, the facts really seem to be the opposite. We observe vices, disputes, and discontent at every level of society, from the highest to the lowest. While we are taught hygiene and correct ways of life in school from childhood to adulthood, we still tend to neglect the rules of a good and decent life and of hygienic and orderly lives.
>
> Current events prove that our society lacks something that, if brought to light and universally recognized, can reshape the present society and bring great happiness and satisfaction to this world. This is the teaching of maximum efficiency and mutual prosperity and benefit (Carlos Gutiérrez García, 2008)".

As it can be observed, the cultivation of moral character promoted through judo by its founder is linked to informal-formal education from the daily processes of its practice, since in this sport we will find, as in others, teachings of etiquette of the sport itself, elements of courtesy in the process of learning and training it, and clear self-control of the subject in their actions to have what we call fair play, on the other hand because its own creator suppressed the dangerous elements of jujitsu, allows on the contrary to what can be assumed support and help with training partners with a high degree of seriousness and teamwork. Here we see the pedagogical process with humanistic sense that Kano imprinted in this sport, the which has been adapted to western criteria, as a path of personal and social progress, used to have a process that generates policies aimed at various meanings as studied in this research.

Judo has had different types of interventions, one of the most important is the educational and social one, its conversion into sport and inclusion as a high performance Olympic sport. "Professor Kano promoted educational reform by highlighting the structure of education, he was responsible for the development of modern physical education and sport in Japan (Jigoro Kano Memorial International Sport Institute, 2020)". Kano, mainly developed sport and education in a holistic way for through this work research and informal education from the perspective of "physical, intellectual and moral (Casado, 2019)", the Jigoro Kano International Sport Institute, puts sport in high esteem in this case Judo implementing activities that favor sport society and values spreading its achievements in four areas:

Research Project

1. Compilation of Kano Jigoro materials and literary analysis.
2. Value of sport in society and its preponderance
3. Historical development of international anti-doping activities and anti-doping education programs.
4. Research visit on anti-doping activities as part of the Olympic Games and Olympic education.
5. The Youth Olympic Games, Singapore 2010 and the development of sports policy in Singapore.
6. The international development of sport and examples of the implementation of activities
7. Development and transformation of the International Olympic Committee and the Olympic Movement

Education Project

1. "Jigoro Kano - Japanese Pioneer in Sports", presents the results achieved through education and sports.
2. Founding member and team administrator of the Olympic Research & Education Center (CORE), in partnership with Tsukuba University.
3. Organize Olympic Education Seminar.

4. Advice for sports education. International

Convention Project

1. Hosting seminars for youth and the Olympic Movement.
2. Organize conferences with presentations given by members of the International Olympic Committee
3. Cooperation for the organization of the World Anti-Doping Agency conference.
4. Administration and organization of the Sport Coaches Forum. International

Development through Sport Project.

1. To support the Kipkeino High School in Kenya, for the promotion of education in sport.
2. Projects of activities related to sports equipment.
3. Send coaches in sports to all Asian and African countries".

In this way, sport is integrated into the social fabric "the space of the dojo is a place of social integration (University of Valencia/FUNDAR / JUDOKAN Valencia, Recovered 2020)" as well as the skills of athletes allowing this link in the tatami and bring it to the community, in addition:

> "In this case, the Kodomo Athletes are part of a process in which they must respect their partners equally, as well as the rules imposed by the Sensei, take care of qualifications, and compete in the tournaments, Being good at home with their parents as well as taking care of the bad things that are good for them, good habits are formed in each one, besides it gives them a lot of pleasure when they win in a tournament so they are made an act of conscience of how they can obtain rewards, for example the medals in the different tournaments, clearly with effort and work" (Luis, 2019).

As a consequence we can observe the good habits and customs generated in the Athletes, which are not only important for them but also for the community, since these young athletes can become a reference for the same, as it happens in other parts of the world where this sport is practiced mainly taking as a reference the European community where:

> "The importance of sport in the social life of Europeans led the European Union to declare 2004 as the Year of Education through Sport (European Commission, 2001). For many years there has been a proliferation of documents and Community or national initiatives that

have tremendous confidence in the potential of sport to help solve major problems in today's society: health, equality, cohesion, integration, and insertion (University of Valencia/FUNDAR / JUDOKAN Valencia, Recovered 2020)".

Consequently, it can be identified that with judo as a high performance sport it creates confidence between the subjects due to the practice of the same, as a reference of the confidence that exists between the teams or members of the Dojos, because in this way it works collaboratively in the mutual progress generating soft competitions in the subjects like socialization, however, as far as the numbers that can be thrown statistically it is complex, because although it is a sport that has taken rise it is not of interest at the moment for the authorities; Rather, it becomes a non-political project for its use, as well as for research, where as a sport it can be verified that through this sport good habits are transferred not only among the athletes, but also among the families and as a consequence in the community, a fact that is perceived with the support that the athletes receive in particular for their community, a fact that can favor the social fabric.

5.- Methodology.

Through the methodology of the research, processes were directed by which they can efficiently reach the status of strategy to achieve concepts, principles and laws that allow to channel an investigation with scientific characteristics, through systematized and structured steps, related to each other to observe an object of study, its characteristics and phenomena, as well as the description of these from various approaches, as is the specific case of this research that has been determined by a qualitative approach and border, this is because it addresses not only various areas mainly being multidisciplinary (education, sport from the criminological vision of crime prevention and security), with high work content

This is a process or work that is carried out mainly outside of the paradigms established by public policy, with a considerably high level of success in terms of the proposals and work carried out in this area: "A simple definition of frontier research could be "those investigations that are developed in the frontiers of knowledge", perhaps qualifying, "in a certain area or field (KING, 2011 recovered 2020)".

5.1.- The Qualitative Look.

For this research, interventions were made that encouraged the participation of the actors from their reality, generating confidence from active listening and group actions, applying diverse dynamics in the training of the athletes to make the acquired knowledge experiential. During the process, comments or reactions relevant to the analysis of risk factors were detected, building a bridge between education-sport-competences-crime prevention, under the perspective of action research, which is that one:

> "undertaken by individuals, groups or communities carrying out a collective activity for the good of all, consisting of a reflective social practice in which theory and practice interact with a view to establishing appropriate changes in the situation under study and in which there is no distinction between what is researched, who is researching and the research process" (Restrepo, 2008).

Thus, this work is a qualitative approach and action research in which the theories of education and criminology are linked in an interdisciplinary way since, "If we want to influence reality, it will be through this action that it will be possible to transform and improve it (Serrano, 2002)", thus contributing, substantially with achievements of purposes and development that encourage the generation of four competencies, knowledge, skills, attitudes and values; it is worth noting that methodologically the definition of crime prevention taken by

The United Nations Office on Drugs and Crime (UNODC), which is linked to the theory of positive general prevention that bases on where it is considered that "crime is indeed a disappointment of expectations (Arechiga, 2017)", so here we can integrate the informal-formal education in a holistic and playful way, seeing in this process the means to lead participants to a new experience with a link in Judo as a high performance sport for crime prevention which at the time:

> "can contribute to the empowerment of the community as a whole, of individuals (especially women and youth) as well as health, education and social inclusion. In particular, sport provides an opportunity for youth groups at risk to develop life skills that enable them to effectively address challenges in their daily lives and move away from their involvement in violence (UNODC, 2019)".

Based on solid principles, individual and group action can be facilitated and promoted in order to evaluate protocols and dimensions of "education and social integration (Ramón Gerardo Navejas Padilla, 2016)", it should be an emic point of view, from the place and with the palpable facts reviewing the topics presented by the subjects and study phenomena, that is why it is important to emphasize that what was indicated by (Patricia Balcazar Nava, 2006) was determined for this work, framed in the following table elaborated by the authors of this product:

1.- It is inductive.	5.- The researcher sets aside his own beliefs; does not However, they are a reference point for studyingthe reality he is studying.	9 .- for this approach, all scenarios and people are worthy of study.	13.-It more oriented towards what is significant, relevantand aware for the participants.
2.-It has a holistic perspective, (perceives	6.-Allperspectives are valuable.	10.-The qualitative researchan art.	14.- it is used in different disciplines,that vandesde the

the person as a whole).			education, sociology, anthropology, psychologyamong others.
3.- There are effects of the researcher onthe people.	7 .- It is considered more than a humanist cut.	11.-Can be appliedto studies in the micro field, since it deepens more in the situation.	15.-Studythe social and cultural organization of a group.
4.-Try to understand people within the framework of reference of themselves.	8.- Emphasis is placed on the validity of the research, close to the empirical world	12.-Signal them aspectsand discrepancies	16 .- is suitable for the analysis of complex phenomena.

In this way, the challenge of this research was investigated and faced, with the purpose of recognizing the work of the Kodomo Dojo and its actors, whose entrepreneurial work seeks through Judo, High Performance Sports as a Pedagogical resource for the Prevention of Crime, in Colonia Constitución, Zapopan, Jalisco, perceptions and challenges because it is urgent to work more than ever.

5.2.- Photography, ethnography, observation and interview

Ethnography has been used for this work, which involved interviewing in a semi-structured and directed manner, observing and describing different aspects such as the characteristics of the colony, photography that "allows for the observation, analysis and theorizing of social reality. More specifically, the image as data helps to contextualize what is observed and makes it possible to go deeper into aspects that are less visible in other ways of recording what is observed (Bonetto, 2016)".

symbolic and material, and the interpretative practices (Duranti, 2000)", when the information was gathered in a direct way it has allowed to obtain truthful comments of the environment, observing the reality, because this is a resource that in a natural way we use every day the human beings to acquire knowledge for that reason it has been used in the work carried out inside this Dojo, and to observe its impact in the conditions that prevail in the same one and the one of the subjects; With this process, the first categories and events have been obtained, such as the actions that prevail on the occasion of training and events of participation of the Dojo and its athletes, for a period of two years. In this way, it has been possible to obtain a relevant record under the premises of non-systemic observation due to the flexibility of the same with reality under the following phases:

1. " Selection of the field of observation.
2. Definition of the aspects within the field to influence the observation process.
3. Establishment of provisional relations between the observed categories and the situations in which they occur, as well as the actions and positions of the actors.
4. Construction of a tentative theoretical explanatory model (Work licensed under a Creative Commons Attribution Non-commercial 3.0 LicenseDepartment of Sociology II. University of Alicante, Recovered 2020)".

Likewise, the application of semi-structured and directed interviews provided elements of freedom with closed and open question processes, obtaining qualitative information in the process of describing information provided by the interviewees.

> "Semi-structured interviews: present a greater degree of flexibility than structured ones, because they start from planned questions, which can be adjusted to the interviewees. Their advantage is the possibility of adapting to subjects with enormous possibilities for motivating the interlocutor, clarifying terms, identifying ambiguities and reducing formalism (Laura Díaz-Bravo, 2013)".

The Colonia Constitución, better known as "*La Consti*" was built in the 60's. This is a popular neighborhood that currently suffers from violence and "Robbery of passers-by, vehicles and homes (Mendoza), 2018)" already in previous work by MORLAN, a company dedicated to the analysis of data from targeted areas, identified social vulnerability or risk factor indices, which can lead to criminal activities, risk variables/factors such as

> " **FAMILY:** Family dysfunction, abuse, conflictive behavior, low supervision, delinquent relatives, lack of cohesion.
>
> **COMMUNITY:** Poverty, presence of drugs and firearms, precarious living conditions, weak neighborhood infrastructure, low social capital
>
> **INDIVIDUAL:** Drug abuse, low motivation, aggressiveness, low level of self-control, low capacity for social interaction
>
> **EDUCATION:** Low performance levels , absenteeism, academic dropout, low motivation, behavioral problems.
>
> **RELATIONSHIPS:** Friends of criminals, relatives in criminal associations, lack of relevant life models (MORLAN, 2014)".

5.3 Photography

Considering the importance and strength of the images, it was considered to document with photography those important semblances by means of cards that identify the follow-up and history in the Kodomo Dojo, as well as by means of catalogs and codes, that revive the observations of key moments transport to value the qualitative work that is developed by means of a semblance with images of the Athletes, these speak for themselves, they tell us doubts, dreams, processes of optimism, hopes, fears, in a word what they are experiencing.

Identification area: Catalogue 1			
Code	Source	Title	Author
0001 Photo 1	Kodomo	Collaborative work	Ramon Gerardo Navejas Padilla

	**Description:** Photo 1.- The little ones areobservedAthletes, helping to provide support in removing the (tatami), training tarpsto clear the work aea at closing during training days.

<table>
<tr><td colspan="4">Identification area: Catalogue 1</td></tr>
<tr><td>Code</td><td>Source</td><td>Title</td><td>Author</td></tr>
<tr><td>0002
Photo 2</td><td>Kodomo</td><td>Socializing</td><td>Ramon Gerardo Padilla Sailing</td></tr>
<tr><td colspan="2"></td><td colspan="2">Description:
Photo 2.- Young athletes chatting after their activity to support the older ones to keep the tatami training canvasesdeveloping skillssoft socializing.</td></tr>
</table>

Identification area: Catalogue 1			
Code	Source	Title	Author
0001 Photo 3	Kodomo	Teamwork	Ramon Gerardo Padilla Sailing
		**Description:** Photo 3.- Team work collecting and storing tatamis is important because the space used is for various disciplines is not an exclusive space for Judo is a Dojo only for training forming responsibility y respect for the following users.	

Identification area: Catalogue 1			
Code	Source	Title	Author
0001 Photo 4	Kodomo	Mutual support	Ramon Gerardo Padilla Sailing
		**Description:** Photo4.- WorkSupportingbetween colleaguesto practice techniques.	

Identification area: Catalogue 1			
Code	Source	Title	Author
0001 Photo 5	Kodomo	Responsi bility	Ramon Gerardo Navejas Padilla
		**Description:** Photo 5.- Leads the young Judoka training, they must learn to take responsibility to lead the younger or lesser grades with respect and harmony.	

Identification area: Catalogue 1			
Code	Source	Title	Author
0001 Photo 6	Kodomo	Judo teaching	Ramon Gerardo Navejas Padilla
		**Description:** Photo 6.- Sensei directs the training helping to perfect the technique of the young athletes.	

<table>
<tr><td colspan="4">Identification area: Catalogue 1</td></tr>
<tr><td>Code</td><td>Source</td><td>Title</td><td>Author</td></tr>
<tr><td>0001
Photo 7</td><td>Kodomo</td><td>Order</td><td>Ramon Gerardo Padilla Sailing</td></tr>
<tr><td colspan="2"></td><td colspan="2">Description:
Photo7 .- Daytraining show of attention and orderbefore the explanation of the techniques that must be used in the corresponding exercise.</td></tr>
</table>

<table>
<tr><td colspan="4">Identification area: Catalogue 1</td></tr>
<tr><td>Code</td><td>Source</td><td>Title</td><td>Author</td></tr>
<tr><td>0001
Photo 8</td><td>Kodomo</td><td>Respect</td><td>Ramon Gerardo Padilla Sailing</td></tr>
<tr><td colspan="2"></td><td colspan="2">Description:
Photo8.- Closingtraining shows respect at all times to his Sensei, farewell greeting.</td></tr>
</table>

<table>
<tr><td colspan="4">Identification area: Catalogue 2</td></tr>
<tr><td>Code</td><td>Source</td><td>Title</td><td>Author</td></tr>
<tr><td>0002
Photo 1</td><td>Kodomo</td><td>Visit</td><td>Ramon Gerardo Padilla Sailing</td></tr>
<tr><td colspan="2"></td><td colspan="2">Description:
Photo 1.-Training day and visit in Kodomo Chapala Jalisco, Dojo for adults, where the young people share trainingand participateinthe activities.</td></tr>
</table>

<table>
<tr><td colspan="4">Identification area: Catalogue 2</td></tr>
<tr><td>Code</td><td>Source</td><td>Title</td><td>Author</td></tr>
<tr><td>0002
Photo 2</td><td>Kodomo</td><td>Respec t or</td><td>Ramon Gerardo Navejas Padilla</td></tr>
<tr><td colspan="2"></td><td colspan="2">Description:
Photo2.-Young athletes respectfully observe how grades are warded to adults.</td></tr>
</table>

<table>
<tr><td colspan="4">Identification area: Catalogue 2</td></tr>
<tr><td>Code</td><td>Source</td><td>Title</td><td>Author</td></tr>
<tr><td>0002
Photo 3</td><td>Kodomo</td><td>Socializ
ation</td><td>Ramon
Gerardo
Navejas
Padilla</td></tr>
<tr><td colspan="2"></td><td colspan="2">Description:
Photo3.-Young athletes socializing with adultsits experience in acquiring knowledgeand recognition as young athletes.</td></tr>
</table>

<table>
<tr><td colspan="4">Identification area: Catalogue 2</td></tr>
<tr><td>Code</td><td>Source</td><td>Title</td><td>Author</td></tr>
<tr><td>0002
Photo 4</td><td>Kodomo</td><td>Team</td><td>Ramon
Gerardo
Navejas
Padilla</td></tr>
<tr><td colspan="2">
</td><td colspan="2">Description:
Photo4 .-Kodomo team respect and order at the end of the training adults with young athletes socializing their experiences.</td></tr>
</table>

<table>
<tr><td colspan="4">Identification area: Catalogue 3</td></tr>
<tr><td>Code</td><td>Source</td><td>Title</td><td>Author</td></tr>
<tr><td>0003
Photo 1</td><td>Kodomo</td><td>Pride</td><td>Ramon
Gerardo
Navejas
Padilla</td></tr>
<tr><td colspan="2">
</td><td colspan="2">Description:
Photo 1.- Young Athlete of Team Kodomo, who achieved after effort and work to beselected to participatein Pan American competition representing to Mexico bythird place Mexicovs USA.</td></tr>
</table>

<table>
<tr><td colspan="4">Identification area: Catalogue 3</td></tr>
<tr><td>Code</td><td>Source</td><td>Title</td><td>Author</td></tr>
<tr><td>0003
Photo 2</td><td>Kodomo</td><td>Achieve
ments</td><td>Ramon
Gerardo
Navejas
Padilla</td></tr>
<tr><td colspan="2"></td><td colspan="2">Description:
Photo 2.- Young athletefrom Kodomo wonthethirdplace, representing Mexico,inthe Panamerican Judo tournament, as a result of personal effort.</td></tr>
</table>

<table>
<tr><td colspan="4">Identification area: Catalogue 3</td></tr>
<tr><td>Code</td><td>Source</td><td>Title</td><td>Author</td></tr>
<tr><td>0003
Photo 3</td><td>Kodomo</td><td>I don't know</td><td>Ramon Gerardo Navejas Padilla</td></tr>
<tr><td colspan="2"></td><td colspan="2">Description:
Photo 3.- Athlete with Senseis, one of the first impressions of this young athlete was "I don't know" the impressions ofevent Representing his countryand belonging to the Kodomo Dojo has impressed him and filled him with pride the work and effort is the sample that this team has achieved with the support of their athletes which shows the teamwork fruit of the effort and continuous work of Sensei Raquel.</td></tr>
</table>

The photography in this research process was a valuable tool to find the daily practices of non-formal education, as well as the learning of various soft skills derived from the sport part to prevent crime as well as and the implementation of non-formal and innovative pedagogical and sports projects that can be used as part of public policy, this exercise has been captured as a project of the Kodomo Dojo, where the passion for sport and education come together to see both personal and team achievements that serve as an example of a community.

5.4 Ethnography

This colony had a market called Bola that was remodeled and transformed into what today is the Constitution Cultural Center and opened on September 21, 2016, a few blocks from a modest gym called Colosso, on the street Obreros de Cananea, this is regularly visited by adults who mainly seek to exercise on bikes or bodybuilding, boxing, zumba; It has two spaces for these sports, one of them is used by the Kodomo Dojo, to practice Judo among the battered tatami, but it is lovingly cared for by the actors and participants of this Dojo, which only has a symbolic charge of $100.00 one hundred pesos a month that basically is to pay the rent of the place, since the instructors do not charge for their services and they are lent the Judoguis, training equipment to the assiduous children, same that new, they have an approximate cost of between $1500.00 thousand five hundred pesos, without charging for the change of ribbon or grade, which makes for many families something accessible because in "other sports such as karate or tae kwon do, charges each grade and is very expensive, "here the teacher does much work with the children what he likes (Family, 2019)" is considered to accept a child in addition to their desire to participate in sport their behavior in the family, their qualifications, and their character in general their behavior, many of them think it but when they arrive and see the environment, that they are welcome, that they are not isolated and that they are involved they take it in a good way and participate; at the beginning of the classes the children put the tatami mats where they train, also at the end of the class they are picked up working in a team in a collaborative way teaching even at this time attitudes and values among their own peers.

5.5 The actors

The actors in this Dojo is divided into three parts: the Sensei or instructors, base of the Dojo with the "sufficient experience at national and international level (Diaz, 2019)" participate three instructors basically "two of them Sensei or Masters, and a young university student seen as the older sister of the practitioners (Q, 2019)", for the purposes of this investigation we will only call "The Sensei", who has carried the mark since the birth of this Dojo; two of the other instructors are guides and figures recognized in the world of judo as national referees of this sport and who support in the conduction of the classes that are distributed in two a week, on Tuesdays and Thursdays, they, the instructors are noteworthy have roots in this colony Constitution, it is also important to say they are graduates of this Dojo, who have found in this sport "skills, attitudes, knowledge and values to such an extent that it is one of the sports that they continue to apply many of the knowledge acquired in daily life (2, 2019)", these young people have managed with diverse vicissitudes to study both engineering at the University of Guadalajara, as well as economic sciences at the same university.

5.6 The athletes.

They are basically primary level children between 6 six to 12 twelve years of age, "there have been up to 25 twenty-five children all from the colony and very few stay to continue the process (Diaz, 2019)", this Dojo contributes greatly to children who suffer some kind of "problem at home school or street is seeking to guide them so they do not get to commit serious offenses to society through this sport (2, 2019)", we already have in the new generations "these

Last already young people of high school and university basically 04 four, adults only for recreational purposes and mobility one (Diaz, 2019)", it is worth highlighting the achievements that this process has had towards the community through a process of working together "family, athletes, Senseis (Mayor, 2019)" with athletes taken to the state podium, In this case, two athletes represented the country in the Pan-American Games. One of these athletes "a girl won third place in her first international exercise, which motivates them to train the second one, who did not win, but still needs to work (Mayor, 2019)":

> "It takes them away from the street and brings them to the dojo even though we do not have much promotion always work for the children of the colony nor do we have support from the municipality even though I have asked them personally by various means for support of a space to promote this sport because of the favorable results we have seen, even by the Zapopan Public Safety Citizen Council, who in a session we attended did not give the support to work and make a tournament in this way to give impulse to this Olympic sport, and to motivate children and families, in that request they returned the subject merely political and said that it was cheaper the soccer, they requested programs that took to the young people of the streets of a day for and of the violence and drugs that said the chief of the police Commissioner, but that cannot be of work, they do not want to work more than in what gives them politically or it makes them see well and thus they did not see the benefits only their political subjects (2 S. , 2019)".

5.7 The families

They live in the surrounding area, and it is the neighbors of this colony who regularly take their children or nephews to practice this sport, so considering the observation proposal where it is stated that "it is susceptible to be applied to any behavior or situation" (Serrano, 2002), it is that the families of the Athletes were observed in the various sports events attending as spectators of their children, grandchildren, nephews, etc. Mainly because in these early stages sport is a bond that teaches a series of skills, for example, working in groups, accepting decisions we do not share, tolerating frustration as it is in a defeat and controlling it.

> "Social actions are the result of what people perceive, understand and interpret of reality, so we must formulate hypotheses or questions that connect the subjective states of people with social action to discover their true meanings" (Bernal, 2010).

Finding a great response from these, not everyone can or wants to compete in state or national sporting events, "my dad says it's too expensive and we have no money (Student, 2019)", this causes that not everyone knows these new processes of life and that many of them consider that their neighborhood is all there is "because to compete, then I can not play in the street with my friends and can not take me, better that way (2 A. , 2018). On the other hand, there is no municipal or institutional support, only those who get this Dojo "are supported and get anonymous sponsors, regularly are people who like this sport, which we have already seen for example with the support for the boys for the Pan-American (Q., 2019)", parents are involved with their children in these sports activities also cultivating not only the love for sport as a means to promote their social relationships, but also as an instrument to prevent crime and to address common situations of everyday life with the skills that are taught with this sport.

5.8 The Municipality

It should be noted that of the programs that exist in terms of crime prevention by the municipality, do not contain activities with this approach, however there are several programs through the Municipal Sports Council Zapopan COMUDE, which on the other hand do not have to do with the approach of study in this work; When you go to their facilities a few steps from the General Commissariat of Public Safety in Zapopan, in the area called the curve whose building is observed with new facilities and a few steps from the baseball stadium Charros de Jalisco, you see how these facilities impose in its renewed structure and within which there is no Judo among the combat sports it promotes are karate, boxing and self-defense. It is worth mentioning that we were referred by the staff to the COMUDE page, where they pointed out that there is a program "nice for the neighborhoods see the page (1, 2019)", having to document from those areas this ethnographic part:

> "It is a program that arises with the need to bring to the colonies, spaces where people can live together, practice some sport or physical activity along with recreational activities, not necessarily within the units that COMUDE administers, but in open spaces where these activities can be carried out: jumping jacks, relay races, mini soccer tournament, dances and exhibitions. This also helps us so that COMUDE schools can carry out a demonstration of their sport, and right there the reports are given so that people can sign up for an initiation school.
>
> "In the playful part we are putting activities like snakes and ladders, giant chess, all this with a movement, so that the child not only develops his mental side, but also has fun, that is the playful part, the game and the fun. The activities are in open spaces so that the snakes and stairs that are commonly known in a board, now play it in a much bigger space so that the child has to move and activate all his systems, so much of the emotional, cardiovascular, the skeletal system and the child has fun (Alba Mireles Torres, Director COMUDE, 2020)".

Similarly, there is little municipal activity for crime prevention work; from the layout and presentation on the current page of this municipality, the strategy of the Municipal President of Zapopan can be seen, in which he emphasizes five basic axes: "education, culture, sports, employment and better health conditions, as a strategy to provide better development conditions (Municipal President Zapopan, 2020)". Where it is indicated that this work is done through models of crime prevention but it does not say what those models are, however it indicates "it seeks to move children and adolescents away from gangsterism, delinquency and addictions and to bring them closer to educational, cultural and sports activities (Municipal President Zapopan, 2020)".

6.- Results.

To obtain results, we worked with the program Atlas.ti, which is a powerful data tool, whose main feature is the interactivity with various file formats, which allowed for rapid crossings of information, we have found that the approach taken by the Kodomo Dojo positions it in social constructivism because it seeks to make social relationships possible to build symbolic networks, both inside and outside the dojo, which are "built in an intersubjective way, creating a context in which discursive practices and their meanings go beyond one's own individual mind (José Manuel Serrano, 2011)", in this way we manage to link the model of pedagogical competencies that are currently handled based on constructivism rescuing as basic elements the following table as a model for crime prevention based on Kodokan Judo Theory and System, which is practiced in the Kodomo Dojo.

Theoretical Body **Knowledge**	The knowledge that is acquired from the discipline and that contains a scientific body
Ethical Spirit **Values**	Based on values, ethical and deontological applicable, experiential; from which a way of living must be made
Physical Training **Skills**	integrates several focuses of interest, through the effective practice of one of its main elements, which is culture as an element of education of the body, mind, and health, in the improvement of the quality of life, and its biomechanical improvement.
Attitudes	Not only of personal satisfaction but also of service to others

Table prepared by the authors with information from (Figueroa, 2004).

The approaches of this pedagogy and Judo make a complete sport, especially as a pragmatic and primordial factor of crime prevention. As we see the importance of the scientific methodology in this sport is necessary because without it the transmission of the competences and of the constructivism would be disarticulated and it would only become a sport centered in the physical part as it is seen by several institutions.

The aim of applying an integrative, complete pedagogy and its methodologies as it is done in Kodomo, shows the great concern and vision of crime prevention and human approach as well as the social responsibility of this institution, without moving away from the traditional concept, without losing his artistic quality and without diminishing the importance of his philosophy and the scientificity of his theory, which "contributes to recovering civility as a subject with all its flats...to be able to collaborate, lend a hand, share (Pagán, 2009)", a fact that is made clear by the list of categories indicated by the athletes themselves, and which here are linked to the competitions in the preceding table from the verbs of Bloom.

KNOWLEDGE	I always learnnew things	The Teacher teaches me	I am correcte d
SKILLS	Controlof the body	I live with my colleagues	I helpto others
ATTITUDES	Happy	Support my colleagues	It's fun
VALUES	Becausemy sister is coming (family bond)	Discipline	Security

Table elaborated with the Kodomo Athletes (athletes of 1, 2019-20)

Thus, the knowledge competence turns into appreciating the capacity of the Athlete to respond to diverse situations that are presented to him in training, as well as to solve problems and to develop in his family, social and educational environment. The skills are important in this sport, these are considered as the capacities that the young athletes have to practice and to do correctly the activity that is asked to them; between such activities we have those that practice and have more knowledge helping in a correct way to those of recent entrance or that have less knowledge thus establishing bonds with the other companions, making collaborative work. The attitude of these athletes is always positive, proactive and enthusiastic, as one of them would say "happy, contented (Athlete, 2019)". Now then, the values must be integrated from the human, ethical and moral aspects, a mold is looked for where an integral being is built with these axiological principles because this is how they become responsible citizens, this is how they make a city, this is how they commit socially from Judo, High Performance Sports as a Pedagogical resource for the Prevention of Crime.

7.- Conclusions.

1.- The vision of having an integrated society is important, so strong ties should be built recovering the social fabric and the quality of good citizen, to achieve such a task is proposed Judo, High Performance Sport as a Pedagogical resource for Crime Prevention, "as an instrument to facilitate the integration of young people (Freire, 2019)", in such a way that young people are socially linked with peers who have the same interests, under programs such as the object of study where it can be faced in an integral manner under the paradigm of competencies, integrated as a strategy with the aspect of criminology whose task is security and crime prevention.

It is considered that the sports vision of the state, does not develop inclusive programs based on sports education to rehabilitate the social fabric or that there are do not cover the integral aspects only cover the sport aspect, some other programs are only an approach to the society that in our social context is seen as insufficient, for that reason it is considered that for the preventive work it is important to consider:

> "Education/prevention and security must be addressed in an integral manner in the strategies of criminal and public policies, and should not be worked on in an autonomous or disjointed manner in the different areas where the institutions will have to do their work from a perspective of social cohesion with processes of Education-Prevention (Ramón Gerardo Navejas Padilla, 2016)".

In such a way that the programs are not adequately oriented or there is no study of their own or method that integrates society.

3 .- It should work on sports and education initiatives, these should aim to prevent crime and above all promote skills under the culture of the model citizen we want, which will help to understand and better address the problems that can hit and undermine society, supporting with collaborative work and proactive participation of society.

8.- Sources.

1. 1, P. m. (September 6, 2019). COMUDE interview. (R. G. Padilla, Interviewer)
2. 2, A. (November 5, 2018). Judo Students. (R. G. Padilla, Interviewer)
3. 2, S. (February 19, 2019). Judo Sensei. (R. G. Padilla, Interviewer)
4. 5, P. (19 of 08 of 2019). Crime Prevention . (R. G. Padilla, Interviewer)
5. Akers, R. L. (1997 pág, 69). *Criminological theories.* Los Ángeles : Roxbury Publishing Company.
6. Alba Mireles Torres, COMUDE Director. (February 19, 2020). *comudezapopan.gob.mx* Retrieved from comudezapopan.gob.mx: https://www.comudezapopan.gob.mx/index.php/programas/moviendo-al-barrio
7. Student. (January 6, 2019). Student 1. (R. G. Padilla, Interviewer)
8. Aréchiga, M. V. (2017). *Bases generales de criminología y política criminal .* Mexico: Oxford.
9. Athlete. (19 of 09 of 2019). Judo. (R. G. Padilla, Interviewer)
10. athletes 1, 3. 4. (various from January - February 2019-20). Interviews Athletes. (R. G. Padilla, Interviewer)
11. Azpúrua Gruber, F. J. (vol. 6, no. 2, July-December, 2005,). The Chicago School. His contributions to social science research. *Sapiens. University Research Journal. ISSN: 1317-5815*, pp. 25-35.
12. Bernal, C. A. (2010). *Research Methodology. Third edition.* Bogotá, Colombia: PEARSON EDUCATION.
13. Bonetto, M. J. (2016). The use of photography in social research. *Latin American Journal of Social Research Methodology: ReLMIS, ISSN-e 1853-6190, No. 11 (Issue devoted to: A FOUR-SIDED TRIANGLE: THEORY, EPISTEMOLOGY, METHODOLOGY AND THE THREAD THAT WEAVES THEM),* 71-83.

14. Carlos Gutiérrez García, M. P. (2008). "The contribution of judo to education" by Jigoro Kano. *Asian Martial Arts Journal, ISSN 1885-8643, Vol. 3, No. 3*, 38-53.

15. Married, J. E. (2019). *Sport and Society Finding the Future of Social and Cultural Studies.* Montevideo Uruguay: Universidad de la Republica de Uruguay.

16. Congress of the Union. (09 of 01 of 2020). *diputados.gob.mx.* Obtained from diputados.gob.mx: http://www.diputados.gob.mx/LeyesBiblio/pdf_mov/Constitucion_Politica.pdf

17. Universal Declaration of Human Rights, Resolution 217 A (III), 10 December 1948 (Adopted and proclaimed by the General Assembly on 10 December 1948).

18. Díaz, R. d. (September 12, 2019). Judo prevention. (R. G. Padilla, Interviewer)

19. Duranti, A. (2000). *Linguistic Anthropology* . Madrid: Cambridge-Madrid: University.

20. Elizabeth, C. L. (2015). *EL ROMPECABEZAS DE LA PREVENCION EN MÉXICO (A Study of Violence and Crime Prevention).* Mexico : University of Xalapa.

21. Family, M. d. (May 6, 2019). Judo sport and costs . (R. G. Padilla, Interviewer)

22. family, P. d. (10 of 12 of 2018). Judo parent interview. (R. G. Padilla, Interviewer)

23. Felipe, G. A. (2007 p.257). *Public Security and Crime Prevention in the Social State of Law. Special commentary on the importance of Education.* Chia Colombia: DÍKAION.

24. Figueroa, N. (2004). *JUDO KODOKAN TEORÍA Y SISTEMA.* United States of America: Boxer Computer Services.

25. Freire, B. E. (2019). *Portraits of Violence* . Mexico: akal.

26. García-Pablo de Molina, A. (1988 Pages 557-559). *Manual of Criminology. Introduction and theories of criminality.* Madrid: Espasa Calpe.

27. Giménez Fuentes-Guerra, F. J., & Rodríguez López, J. M. (2006). LOOKING FOR THE EDUCATIONAL SPORT HOW TO TRAIN THE TEACHERS? *Challenges. New trends in Physical Education, Sport and Recreation,* 40-45.

28. Government of Mexico. (January 4, 2020). *Ministry of Public Education* . Obtained from Secretaría de Educación Pública : https://www.dgespe.sep.gob.mx/reforma_curricular/planes/lepri/plan_de_estudios/enfoque_centrado_competencias

29. Habitat for Humanity in Mexico (19-02-20 of Recuperado de 2018). *habitatmexico.org.* Retrieved from habitatmexico.org: https://www.habitatmexico.org/article/el-tejido-social

30. Report on Citizen Security and Human Rights , OEA/Ser.L/V/II. Doc. 57 (Inter-American Commission on Human Rights, 31st of December 2009).

31. National Electoral Institute-El Colegio de Mexico. (2015). Country Report on the Quality of Citizenship in Mexico. In I. N.-E. Mexico, Informe país sobre la *calidad de la ciudadanía en México* (p. 16). Mexico: Infagon web, S.A. de C.V. .

32. Jigoro Kano Memorial International Sport Institute (05 of 03 of 2020). *Jigoro Kano Memorial International Sport Institute.* Obtained from Jigoro Kano Memorial International Sport Institute: http://100yearlegacy.org/sp/Kano_Jigoro/pdf/kj_panph_Spanish.pdf

33. José Manuel Serrano, R. M. (2011). Constructivism today: constructivist approaches in education. *Electronic Journal of Educational Research,* https://redie.uabc.mx/redie/article/view/268/708.

34. Laura Diaz-Bravo, U. T.-G.-H.-R. (2013). Research methodology in medical education. The interview, a flexible and dynamic resource. *Research in medical education On-line version ISSN 2007-5057,* Investigación educ. médica vol.2 no.7 México jul./sep.

35. Luis, 0. S. (November 9, 2019). Kodomo Judo . (R. G. Padilla, Interviewer)

36. Mayor, I. H. (December 12, 2019). Judo . (R. G. Padilla, Interviewer)

37. Mendoza), J. A. (May 12, 2018). Gangs lurk in the streets of 'La Consti'. *El Diario.com. critical journalism,* page https://www.ntrguadalajara.com/post.php?id_nota=98632.

38. Merton, R. K. (2002). *Teoría y estructuras sociales, Introducción de Mario Bunge.* Mexico: Fonde de Cultura Económica.

39. MORLAN. (19 February 2014). *MORLAN,MX.* Obtained from MORLAN.MX: http://www.morlan.mx/zapopan/

40. Work placed under Creative Commons Attribution Non-commercial license 3.0 LicenseDepartment of Sociology II. University of Alicante (01 de

March 2019 of Recovered 2020). *Social Research Techniques.* Obtenido de Tecnicas de Investigación Social: https://sites.google.com/site/tecninvestigacionsocial/temas-y- contenidos/tema-4-las-tecnicas-estructurales-entrevista-grupo-de-discusion-observacion-y-biografia/tecnicas-de-observacion-no- sistematica

41. Orellana Wiarco, O. (2007). *Manual of Criminology 11th edition.* Mexico: Porrúa .

42. Pagán, J. B. (2009). *Educating in troubled times.* Barcelona: GRAÓ DE IRIF, S.L:.

43. Patricia Balcazar Nava, N. I.-A.-F. (2006). *Qualitative Research.* Mexico: Universidad Autonoma del Estado de Mexico.

44. Municipal President Zapopan. (February 19, 2020). *https://www.zapopan.gob.mx/apuesta-zapopan-por-modelos-de-prevencion- del-delito/.* Retrieved from https://www.zapopan.gob.mx/apuesta-zapopan-por-crime-prevention-models/: https://www.zapopan.gob.mx/apuesta-

45. Q., M. (October 12, 2019). Family Judo. (R. G. Padilla, Interviewer)

46. Ramón Gerardo Navejas Padilla, D. H. (2016). *Citizen participation in public policies of prevention and security in the municipalities of the State of Jalisco.* Mexico: CONACYT AND OTHERS.

47. Royal Academy of the Spanish Language. (09 of 09 of 2020). *Dictionary of the Spanish Language.* Retrieved from Diccionario de la Lengua Española: https://dle.rae.es/deporte

48. Restrepo, C. c. (2008). ACTION RESEARCH. A heuristic methodological tool for the understanding and transformation of realities and socio-educational practices. *Laurus, vol. 14, no. 27, May-August, 2008*, 92-114.

49. REY, J. (March 21, 2011 recovered 2020). *Fundación General CSIC.* Obtained from Fundación General CSIC: http://www.fgcsic.es/lychnos/es_es/tribuna/investigacion_de_frontera_traer_un_futuro_al_presente

50. Ruiza, M. F. (n.d.). *The online biographical encyclopedia.* Retrieved September 02, 2020, from https://www.biografiasyvidas.com/biografia/k/kano_jigoro.htm

51. Sahagún, L. A. (2008). *Citizenship and Profession Elements for an Ethics of Coexistence* . Mexico: Temacilli.

52. Serrano, G. P. (2002). *Qualitative Research Challenges and Questions II. Techniques and data analysis.* Madrid: Muralla.

53. TIEGHI, O. 1.-3. (1989 Pages 388-389). *Treatise on Criminology.* Buenos Aires: University, Buenos Aires,.

54. University of Chile/Open Society Institute/Center for Citizen Security Studies. (01 of 10 of 2004). *cesc.uchile.cl.* Obtained from cesc.uchile.cl.: http://cesc.uchile.cl/publicaciones/com_y_prev_01.pdf

55. University of Valencia/FUNDAR / JUDOKAN Valencia. (09 de 05 de Recuperado 2020). *programajudokan.* Obtained from Program of socio-educational integration through Judo 2011: http://www.programajudokan.com/g1_3.htm

56. UNODC. (December 30, 2019). *UNODC Doha.* Retrieved from UNODC Doha: https://www.unodc.org/dohadeclaration/es/topics/crime-prevention- through-sports.html

57. UNODOC/United Nations Office on Drugs and Crime/International Centre for the Prevention of Crime. (2011). *Manual on the effective implementation of the Guidelines for the Prevention of Crime.* New York: United Nations.

58. W, A. H. (reissued March 2020). *Risk factors and juvenile delinquency, review of national and international literature* Santiago de chile : Fundación Paz ciudadana.

59. World Justice Project. (report 2018, 2019, 2020). *Index of the Rule of Law in Mexico.* Washington D.C.: World Justice Project.

More Books!
yes

MIX
Papier aus verantwortungsvollen Quellen
Paper from responsible sources
FSC® C105338

FSC
www.fsc.org

Printed by Books on Demand GmbH, Norderstedt / Germany